The Glory of Kings

An Invitation to Special Needs Pastoring

By Rochelle Beckemeyer

TRILOGY
PROFESSIONAL PUBLISHING MEETS POWERFUL PROMOTION

A wholly owned subsidiary of TBN

The Glory of Kings: An Invitation to Special Needs Pastoring
Trilogy Christian Publishers a Wholly Owned Subsidary of Trinity
Broadcasting Network
2442 Michelle Drive Tustin, CA 92780

Rights Department, 2442 Michelle Drive, Tustin, CA 92780.
Trilogy Christian Publishing/TBN and colophon are trademarks of Trinity Broadcasting Network.
For information about special discounts for bulk purchases, please contact Trilogy Christian Publishing.

Manufactured in the United States of America
10 9 8 7 6 5 4 3 2 1
Library of Congress Cataloging-in-Publication Data is available.

B-ISBN#: 978-1-68556-042-3
E-ISBN#: 978-1-68556-043-0

Acknowledgements

Thanks to my pastoral coach, Dave Jacobs from Small Church Pastor; Dave's encouragement and ideas have helped our ministry to become what it is, and without his cajoling and coaxing, I would not have even considered moving forward with writing a book!

Thanks to Pastor Kevin Carpenter; his leadership and pastoral care during the coffee shop days were just what they needed to be to prepare me for this marvelous work.

Thanks to my mom and dad, whose unwavering love and support are felt not only by me but by all in the congregation; they are "Mom" and "Dad" to us all, helping to make Echo a true family!

Thanks to each and every one of those mentioned in these pages; without their courage to embrace who God made them to be, there wouldn't be anything for me to write. Special thanks to "Michelle" (you know who you are) whose steadfast encouragement has been a great blessing, and whose suggestion to consider Trilogy Publishing got this ball rolling. Special thanks also to Lila whose great faith and courage challenges me to keep going.

Thanks also to those who have supported and encouraged this work along the way: Regie Holloway, John and Sheila Belkowski, Toni Ufolla, Penny Shults, Michele Smither, Melissa Carpenter, Jim and Lori Greco, Roger Steed, Rob

Longo, Mary Makarewicz, and the saints at LakePoint Community Church and Auburn Hills Christian Center, and of course, my Schmoopie, the best daughter in the world!

Finally, above all and over all, *merci* Jesus for Your great, great love, for Your passion for this little flock, and for letting us catch a glimpse of the glorious treasure Your Spirit has planted in each and every one of Your people.

Table of Contents

Foreword

"Recently, our culture has started the process of recognizing and responding to marginalized people groups. One such group that is still low on the list are those described as "special needs adults," or people with mental or physical limitations. This neglect is seen not only in the secular world but also in the church world. Reaching and accommodating these special children of God means more than simply installing a wheelchair ramp for one's church building.

How can we make special needs people truly feel welcomed, valued, and included in our churches?

Pastor and author Rochelle Beckemeyer is one of the few voices who can speak from years of fruitful experience in leading a church made up predominantly by people living with emotional and physical limitations. This is her story and the story of her special people. It is my expectation that this short book will be a source of inspiration and motivation for many churches to begin asking how they can get better at embracing this large segment of society."

Dave Jacobs, Author and Leadership Coach

"Rochelle and Echo Christian Fellowship serve a segment of the population that is often overlooked and under-served. The blessings and honesty that this congregation brings to all who know them is captured in her book. The stories made me smile."

Michele Smither, Dutton Farm Co-Founder

Introduction

"It is the glory of God to conceal a matter,
But the glory of kings is to search out a matter."

Proverbs 25:2

Once upon a time, I served under the leadership of a pastor whose passion for the Word of God inspired us to spend hours digging for God's buried treasures in Scripture, especially in what seemed like obscure passages. With Proverbs 25:2 as our banner, we would revel in the glory of the chase, searching out matter after matter. Huddled around our Bibles and laptops at a local coffee shop, we would hunt for as long as it took to be satisfied with some application, some revelation, some practical knowledge of our awesome God. Oh, those were the days! I have often wondered whatever happened to having all that time for study. Now that I'm also serving as a bivocational senior pastor, I still study devotionally and for sermons, but I just don't seem to devote as much time to it as in the past.

I recently realized, however, that my hunting days are far from over. I have still been seeking and finding God's glory in His Word, but more and more I have been finding great treasure hidden right where the Apostle Paul said we'd find it: within the "earthen vessels" around us (2 Corinthians 4:7). By this, of course, I mean people, and just as we used to search out seemingly obscure passages of Scripture,

I have taken particular delight in searching out marginalized people, "hunting" in a field that seems to others to be barren, empty, or just too difficult and unyielding. What treasure hunter worth his salt, though, doesn't get excited to discover areas where no one else has been looking? Who wouldn't be willing to get their hands (and knees, elbows, clothing, and interior of their car) dirty to dig in such a field? Who wouldn't be willing to maybe break a few fingernails and endure a few frustrations and humiliations at the prospect of uncovering great and glorious treasure that might have otherwise been missed?

Well... maybe not everyone is that hungry for a good treasure hunt, and that's okay! If you are up for the challenge, though, allow me to suggest a field like mine, where there's *a lot* of room to dig and a great deal of value to be uncovered. The field I'm talking about is known as special needs ministry, including those with brain disorders referred to as mental illnesses.

In this book, I invite you to experience some fairly typical real-life ministry among our people who live with various disabilities. Each chapter describes moments in a given day along with observations and lessons learned. There are five weekdays highlighting the glory I've been fortunate to see in various individuals, followed by a weekend containing a church service and a day of rest (because self-care is crucial!). In the final chapter, I provide some ideas you might find helpful for starting or enhancing your own ministry.

Are you ready to dig? Let's go!

Day 1: Ministry of Presence

8:30 a.m.

There's a tap on my shoulder. I lean away from my computer screen, and George takes a step back, wide-eyed with some question or other on his mind, not really wanting to speak and disrupt the quiet but not quite able to keep his thoughts to himself. I stretch while I smile my encouragement up at him. The day's just starting, and I have lots of work ahead of me, but I can break for a few minutes. "What's up, George?"

"Yeah, Rochelle? Yeah, so I've been thinking...and I have a question."

"Okay, sure. Go ahead."

"How become, how become..." Although I can't remember this day's question, our conversations frequently start this way, and his questions are almost always about guardianships, the legal system, or how people abuse authority. I share some basic insight, nothing earth-shattering, and he explains his own view and why he was thinking about it. It's generally related to some hurt that he's remembering and processing, and it seems to bring him comfort to talk about it in a safe environment. It ends with him expressing pity for the person who mistreated him, because he figures that they were probably suffering. He then goes on his way, and I turn back to the computer.

10:15 a.m.

George quietly approaches, reaches around me to pick up my coffee cup and take it away for a refill. I've never asked him to do it, but he does it anyway. "Thanks, George!" A minute or so later, after thinking carefully about his response, or maybe just lost in a reverie and suddenly remembering he's supposed to respond, he replies: "You're welcome!"

11:30 a.m.

I'm on a conference call when George heads my way with an open book in his hand. I can see he wants to share something he's read, but I hold up a hand and point to my earpiece. He nods and backtracks to some other part of the house. I don't remember this exchange until later, as I'm typing these notes. I determine to ask him tomorrow about what he read.

1 p.m.

"Hey Rochelle?"

"Yep."

"I did my laundry and used a sponge to clean up some sticky spots on the floor."

"Great job, George."

"Okay."

Off he goes.

6:30 p.m.

As I start closing applications to end the workday, I call out for George.

"Yeah, Rochelle?"

"Want to go for a walk?"

"Yeah."

We head out to circle the neighborhood where George lives. A block or so from his home, we see a mom and a dad and two extra-cute kids in their front yard. We're still new in town, so we introduce ourselves. Dad's name is Dan.

"Hey, Dan? Can I ask you a question?" This is George's way of socializing.

"Sure," says Dan, looking only a tiny bit apprehensive.

"Do you watch baseball?"

I realize George has noticed that Dan's wearing a Detroit Tigers cap. Within a few minutes Dan and his family get to know George in his thoughtful, inquisitive, sweet, and delightful glory. We walk away; George a little sad about the season being halted (this is in the middle of June 2020, and the whole world's gone on pause for the COVID-19 virus). As we approach his home and my office, George tells me he really hopes the league managers don't expect all those players to just be okay without being paid for the whole season.

8 p.m.
George and I hold hands and pray before I leave for the day.

Life as George's guardian is a series of sweet moments like these. Are there times he needs reminding to clean up?

Sure. Is he prone to leaving his room a little scattery? You bet. On the whole, though, he really is a delight. I tell him he is not just my ward, he's my "REward" for enduring hardships in other areas of ministry. He gets a chuckle out of that. More than once, he's told me that, even if I sometimes forget to do things for him or it takes me a long time to get him the things he needs, he's always going to be pretty happy with me as long as we get to talk.

Herein lies the first principle I'd like to share with you, and it's the first and possibly most powerful and most freeing lesson I learned in ministry among people with special needs. This ministry, and ministry in general, doesn't require that you first learn to do everything perfectly or completely. It really just requires that you show up. You see, "God sets the lonely in families" (Psalm 68:6); many of those with disabilities, especially when coupled with mental illness, are profoundly lonely. They often have a surprisingly good understanding of the elements of our faith; what they long for is the simple living out of that faith in relationship. What we can do is just be there and be family.

I'm reminded of the first time taking one of our other people, Mary, out for a shake at McDonald's. She had been asking and asking and asking, and finally I agreed. I admit now that I was dreading the visit, not because of Mary (who really is very sweet), but because I didn't know what to say or how to minister to her. Insecurity based on feeling ill-equipped to do a task does have a way of robbing us of joy, doesn't it? I was used to deep spiritual conversations and intense Bible studies, but how do you get there with someone who has some obvious cognitive limitations? What do you talk about, anyway?

Well. She taught me a lesson that day. Mary was just so happy to be out with someone. It's humbling to realize that she really would have been happy with anybody. She wasn't expecting a whole lot out of me, only that I was kind and polite and would sit and enjoy a shake with her. I had thought that this outing would somehow fall short of what we call "ministry," but instead, I found a deep satisfaction in doing this simple thing that day, and a sense that this was God's will in this ordained moment. There was also tremendous peace, a relief that this ministry doesn't require a lot of skill or knowledge, just some patience and presence. It was then that I was hooked, and I still experience that satisfaction and peace regularly. It helps to sustain me for the rough times… and yeah, there are rough times.

Cue Day 2…

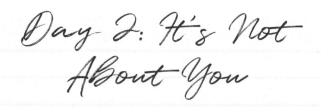

Day 2: It's Not About You

5:39:05 a.m.

My Phone (on silent): *FLASH* for a new text message

Me: *SNORE*

5:39:48 a.m.

Phone: *FLASH* for another new text message

Me: *SNORE*

5:41 a.m.

Phone: *FLASH* for another new text message

Me: *SNORE*

(This sequence is repeated at 5:42am, 5:43am, 5:45am, 5:46am, 5:47am, 5:49am, and 5:53am.)

5:58 a.m.

Me (stretching and yawning and looking at my phone): O Lord, help me...

When the day starts like this with Abby, I have some choices to make. I can 1) Call right away, 2) Call a little later when I'm sufficiently caffeinated, 3) Call much later, or 4) Ignore the whole thing (this really is an option!). If and when I call, I then have more choices: 1) Yell at her for being upset that I didn't respond while I was *sleeping*, 2) Calmly and gently find out how I can help, or 3) Act like I don't know that the texts were filled with angry f-bombs and say, "Hey, what's up?" On a good day, I remember to pray before I do anything. I pray for wisdom in how to help, and if I'm having a really good day spiritually, I'll pray for her because she's been in a manic state for months with little help from anyone. I'll remember that most people have been alienated by her, and their abandonment, while understandable for their own health and sanity, has left her feeling very isolated. She's obviously in a rough spot, and her vitriol, while technically aimed at me, isn't really meant for me.

Because you see…it's not about me.

I don't remember this truism very well today, however.

6:04 a.m.
I call Abby, barking that I just woke up and asking what on earth she could possibly want that was so urgent. The call lasts six minutes. I don't remember what was said, only that I don't feel very smart afterward, and I know it was a mistake to call when I did. *Sigh.* I roll on with my day.

12:36 p.m.
Text to Danny: "I'll be there about 1:15 to pick up for Dr"

1:16 p.m.
I'm a minute late, not too bad. Danny, forty-three going on sixteen, runs out of the house with red and blue

streamers attached to his bicycle knee pads and an American-flag-sequined fedora over his long bleach-blond hair with pink extensions. He's got quite the ensemble going on today, including his favorite pink form-fitting t-shirt with "Babe" emblazoned across the chest, and new pink sequined sunglasses to finish off the look. He jumps in, making loud noises about hurting his knee and how his wife is killing him about cigarettes. Joanna, his tiny, rail-thin wife, twenty-five years his senior and looking every minute of it, is slowly making her way to the car with a little smile on her face. Danny launches himself out of the car and back into the house. He bolts back outside moments later, and now he's got a problem: he's locked both bedroom keys in the bedroom and wants me to do... what, I'm not exactly sure. Something to do with a screwdriver. I explain I don't have much experience with breaking and entering. Joanna giggles. "Never mind, never mind," he retorts. "You don't understand my English." He throws himself into the car in a huff and off we go.

2:20 p.m.
I drop Joanna off at her 2 p.m. appointment, making a mental note for next time that forty-five minutes is not enough time to get them to an appointment ten minutes away.

2:45 p.m.
While checking in Danny at his appointment, he keeps mentioning his wife and his God-wife. I'm only half-listening because I'm trying to look up the name of the doctor who placed the order for today's tests. I come up with it finally, and Danny confirms the name, turns

to the nurse and states that his God-wife (gesturing to me) usually takes care of that information. God-wife? "Oh, no, no-no-no, Danny..." But he and the nurse have moved on, and neither is really interested in setting the record straight. We're not here for me, anyway; this is Danny's appointment.

That's right, it's still not about me.

In ministry, especially among the mentally ill, it's extremely important to learn those words. Say them with me: It's. Not. About. Me.

This applies to the many times we have to choose not to take things personally or not to protect our image, and it also applies to how we think about ministering to the mentally ill. For instance, when the topic of difficult people comes up among pastors, many will advise some form of avoidance. We justify blocking difficult people because we are responsible for protecting our families, the rest of the flock, and our own mental health. We figure it's right and healthy and downright humble to acknowledge that we, like most pastors, are not equipped to treat severe mental illness.

What if, however, we realized that our interactions with the mentally ill don't all have to be focused on treatment? What if the point isn't for us to be their solution? If it's really not about us, then we can freely embrace them (carefully, of course, and maybe not literally) and walk alongside as friends and encouragers on the road. Maybe they need professional help, maybe they even need hospitalization, and maybe we can help them get treatment. What they for *sure* need, though, is a friendly face and a warm smile. They need tiny gestures of kindness and respect. They surely need to know about Jesus, and when they feel safe enough to sit still during a service, they will listen to and engage with the Word. They also need people who will just be there, on their side, when everyone else is disgusted or frustrated or tired. We won't be the ones to fix them, and we can't be present all the time, but we can be human, and choose to see and treat these people as humans. We can do small things and let God do the big stuff.

After all, it's not about us doing something huge for God.

Remember, it's not about you, and it's not about me!

Now, I can't leave this chapter and this day without highlighting some of the glory that makes it worth it (because it's also not just about enduring difficult behavior!).

5:45 p.m.
Finally, we pull up in front of Danny and Joanna's house. Danny has bounded up the porch steps before Joanna has her car door open, but by the time I've given her a hug (ever so gently, considering her brittle frame), Danny's back with a bottle of cold water.

"Here you go, Pasture!" That's not a typo. I don't know why, but I have always been "Pasture" to him.

"Thanks, Danny!"

"Uh-huh. Need your trash taken out? Any empties to get rid of?"

"No, thanks Danny, have a good night. Love you!"

"Okay, love you too!" He twirls away to show off his streamers some more, and I give him a thumbs-up before I drive away, enjoying my water and remembering what Jesus said:
"For whoever gives you a cup of water to drink because of your name as followers of Christ, truly I say to you, he will not lose his reward" (Mark 9:41).

11:52 p.m.
Phone: *FLASH* for a new text message
Me: *SNORE*

The new message from Abby reads: "Hey Pasta Rochelle LOL good night and God bless!"

It's a good thing I'm not hung up on being called "Pastor" because, that's right, it's not about me!

Day 3: Things Aren't Always as They Seem

11:30 a.m.
Joy shuffles to the car and climbs in with no assistance. She settles in and gives a little self-satisfied smile. "Did you see that? I climbed in by myself."
"Yep," I respond. "All by your big girl self!" I start the car and say, as I often do, "... and we're off!"
Joy adds, as she often does, "...like a herd of turtles!"

This year alone, Joy has been the subject of at least a dozen 911 calls, followed by emergency room visits. So far today, though, she looks good, ready to take in some retail therapy, and I'm happy to check items off of my own ever-present to-do list.

12:05 p.m.
Joy's calmly playing a video game on her phone while lying on an emergency room bed. Chest pains and dizziness have cut our errands short, so we'll be spending the time at the hospital instead.

Things really aren't always as they seem! I think medical professionals and caregivers must learn very early that what we see with our eyes is often just a small portion of everything that is happening with an individual. I'm learning this lesson by hanging out with Joy.

Joy has a quiet happiness about her that goes beyond her circumstances. She's almost always ready with a smile, has a quick sense of humor, and especially loves to tease and be teased. Under the surface, though, there are many medical and emotional issues that require treatment, monitoring, and plain old hounding to make sure sugar levels and medications are managed properly. She may seem okay, but then… suddenly she's not!

'This notion, of course, applies to emotional issues even more than medical issues. While waiting to see a doctor, Joy tells me that several people from her peer group had contacted her the day before. It turns out she hadn't heard from any of them since the COVID-19 pandemic started. She had reached out and left messages regarding her hospitalizations, but no one had called her back. Everyone assumed she was fine, but she says she was really hurt by it and didn't say anything until it finally made her mad enough to post on the group's social media page. This resulted in the phone calls, and she says that made her happy.

I tell this story to show how easy it is to assume people are fine emotionally, when they actually aren't. What then can we do? I don't think this means we need to hold ourselves responsible for everyone's happiness or run ourselves ragged trying to make sure everyone feels seen and loved every moment of every day. I do think, however, that we can be aware that there's more going on with people than we can see, and we can be patient and loving and responsive if and when those hidden feelings come to the surface.

11:55 p.m.
A call comes in from the hospital where I thought Joy was being admitted. They are ready for me to pick her up, as evidently, she's fine. As I pull on my shoes, I ponder another side to this lesson: things aren't always as bad as they seem, either!

This truth also applies to emotional issues. If someone has a blow-up, it's not the end of the world; they will generally come back down, and if you stay the course and don't let it scare you off, you get to see and be part of the healing process. And that, my friend, is worth the rollercoaster ride, I promise!

Day 4: Odds Exist to Be Beaten

10 a.m.
Cleaning out old voicemails, I come across one from 2015 that I'll never delete:

From 2/8/2015, 5:15 p.m.
"(Sigh) Hello Pastor Rochelle, I got something to tell you... It's a very hard decision for me to make but I prayed about it. Um... I don't feel so good about it, in my heart, but... it's probably the best thing for me to do, and it's probably the right thing for me to do...but... if you can get the paperwork in order, I will sign it for Sabrina to be adopted. Alright. Love you bye."

Every time I listen to it, I'm in awe of what God has done in Lila, back then and now. When I first met her in 2011, I was dropping off some groceries because her mom had asked me to. Lila's daughter Sabrina, then eleven, had attended church a few times, but I hadn't met Lila yet. Lila told me that she didn't really do the church thing, not since she was little, and she was upset with her mom for calling me. "Thanks, anyway," she said, and insisted that she was fine. I left, but not before I prayed for her and invited her to a fall outing that was coming up.

Over the next two years, Lila did slowly start attending worship with us, and I learned about her issues with bipolar disorder, depression, past drug abuse, and current abuse of her medications. In 2013, knowing her life was out of control, she agreed to place herself in a residential treatment facility. Her brother came to get Sabrina, taking her into his home and becoming her guardian.

When Lila came out of treatment, she was surprised to learn that the guardianship came with conditions that she would have to meet in order to get Sabrina back. The list of conditions was overwhelming, and though Lila worked on them, she never was able to complete all of them. Within a year, Sabrina came to live with me because the circumstances with her uncle changed, and she could no longer stay there. Meanwhile, Lila got picked up for shoplifting, and opted for jail time instead of going on parole. Parole came with another set of requirements that she knew she couldn't meet, and she decided she would rather just get locked up and get it over with.

It was during her time in jail that she started reading the Bible and really growing in her relationship with God. As she tells it, "When I first went in, I was just looking forward to getting out again and doing the stupid stuff I was doing before. But while I was there, all that changed, and when I left, I had no desire at all to do any of it anymore." Jailhouse conversions are common, but people often backslide once they return to the community, especially when they return to the same circumstances as they were in prior to their conversion. Against the odds, Lila's transformation proved to be genuine, with friends and family surprised to see her distance herself from situations that used to trigger bad decisions. Lila's spiritual growth was put to the test in 2015 when she was asked whether she would agree to my adopting Sabrina. The court would not have required Lila's consent to proceed, but we really felt like it was important to give her that opportunity. Initially, she said no because she didn't think adoption was necessary; she didn't have any plans to make Sabrina come back to her. She wanted her back but also knew a fight wouldn't be worth it, and she probably wouldn't regain her custody. Then, a few weeks later, I received that voicemail from Lila, and on July 13, 2015, Sabrina was adopted, with Lila standing up in court to give her agreement. The odds were really against this happening, but it did!

It's almost like odds exist just to be beaten.

10:31 a.m.
Phone: *FLASH*
A new text message comes in while I'm still looking at my phone, having listened to that voicemail a couple more times. I wipe away my tears of gratitude and see that the message is from Lila. Go figure!

"Good morning I need directions to your house so when I get ready to go over there I'll have it. I should be there probably about 1:30, 1:40."

Today, she's driving Joy (remember her from yesterday?) to a doctor's appointment, and they're planning to stop by my house afterward to help me with some paperwork. Lila's still clean, growing in her faith and serving the community every chance she gets. She's always quick to pray for others and to invite them to church, and, come to think of it, to bring them food. We've come full circle from our initial encounter!

As I consider the many odds Lila has beaten, I think of others in the church who have also overcome against all expectations.

Take Lila's mother, Wilma, for instance, the one who sent me to Lila's house with food. Wilma is legally blind and has lived with a brain tumor for decades and was told she should have died a long time ago, but she grins and stands with her fists on her hips, saying, "God has other plans! He helps me to lead people who can see!" Indeed, it's like odds exist to be beaten!

Then there's Sabrina, who was in and out of foster care before she went to her uncle's home. She was in a special education program because she was struggling to understand most subjects, but I suspected her issues were more related to focus, feeling safe at home, and getting help when she needed it. When she moved in, I asked her, "Do you know what your job is?" She answered, "Well, I got fired from my last job!" You see, she really thought her job was to take care of her mom! I told her that her job was to be a student, and she took it to heart. Five years later, she graduated high school, having mainstreamed out of the special education program.

This year, she earned a college degree in mental health and social work and is employed as a night shift caregiver to foster children. She also serves as president of the board of Safe & Sound Ministries, our nonprofit corporation created to help improve the quality of life for individuals with mental illness and/or cognitive disabilities. Considering where she came from, many would say the odds were against her from the beginning, but yes, odds exist to be beaten!

Oh, and remember Danny and Joanna? Before I became their guardian, they were living in an abandoned house because they didn't want to live in the group homes where they'd been placed. I asked them what they wanted, and they said, "We want to be married and live together!" I figured, "Well, why not?" I know their little family unit isn't conventional, and they do need help taking care of medical and financial business, but, against expectations, there they are, married and living together. Odds of this happening? Eh, odds, shmodds...

I could go on and on. One common denominator in all these stories is our willingness to ignore the odds and just try things out, giving people space and encouragement to grow however they are made to grow. Sometimes there are special qualities that manifest when people are allowed to grow around the obstacles in their lives, similar to how trees that have experienced trauma or sickness will develop these magnificent bends and curves. People may surprise you with how they overcome odds if you give them a chance and don't let the odds scare you.

1:36 p.m.

Phone: *FLASH* There's a new text message from Lila:

"Hello we are here at the doctors."

Following the message is an image of a fuzzy bear with his arms stretched out wide and the words "A BIG HUG FOR YOU!" written across his belly.

If you had told me back in 2011 that I'd be getting cute, hugging-bear messages from this lady who wanted nothing to do with me and my church and my prayer and my groceries, I'd have said the odds were against that happening. Yes, well… we know what we've learned about odds, don't we?

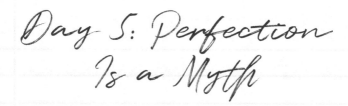

Day 5: Perfection Is a Myth

10:32 a.m.

Phone: *FLASH* silently, notifying me of an incoming call. I glance at the number, do a mental calculation of time left before my next meeting, and decide I can pick up.

Me: "Hello?"

Recorded Voice: "Hello! You have a call at no expense to you from... "

Pamela: "Pamela"

Recorded Voice: "...an inmate at Oakland County Jail. To accept this call, press or say 5. To refuse this call, hang up now. To block this call and all future calls, press or say 9."

Me: *tapping on 5* "Hi there!"

Pamela: "Hi Pastor! How are you? Are you good?"

Me: "Yep, doing okay, thanks Pamela. How are you?"

Pamela: *sighing* "I'm okay... Thanks for the Bible and coloring books."

Me: "You're welcome. Is there anything else I can send?"

Pamela: "Yeah, if you can, if it's not too much trouble..."

Me: "Sure!"

Pamela: "People magazine, Bible word searches, anime coloring books?"

Me: "You got it!"

Pamela: "Do you want to pray?"

Me: "I'd love to!"

I pray a short prayer for her, for peace, for favor, for protection. She then prays for me, a beautiful petition for God's glory to shine through me and also for Him to keep me safe and strong.

Pamela's going to court today to hear the results of her competency hearing. If declared competent to stand trial, she will get a pre-trial date and will probably plead guilty. By the time she's sentenced, most of that sentence will already be served, and before I know it, she'll be home again.

This isn't Pamela's first time around this particular block, nor is it my first time around with her. I wish I could say things are getting better, but right now, it really doesn't look like they are, at least not on the surface. Pamela's story would sound made-up if I didn't know for a fact that it's real. Born with a cognitive disability to a crack-addicted mother, she was removed at a young age and shuffled around foster care where she was abused physically and sexually. By the time she hit her twenties she was addicted to drugs, and by the time she made it to her thirties, she had already given birth and lost custody to two children. She met and married another addict, and together they got married, got clean, and had two beautiful children. Fade out, queue the uplifting swell of music and roll the credits...

I wish I could say that's all, I really do, but the story goes on.

When their children were one and two years old, there was an accident in the home. Pamela stepped on a small, light plastic toy and hurt her foot, then tossed the toy behind her into the living room where her son was playing quietly, closer to the door than she realized. She didn't see the toy hit him, but she heard him start crying, and turned to see a cut on his lip. It's still not clear whether it was the toy that hit him, or that the thrown toy started a chain of events that led to him bumping his lip. At any rate, Pamela immediately scooped up the kids and took them to urgent care, where the boy received a few quick stitches. The doctor was incredulous when he heard the story, and didn't know how this toy could have caused the injury. Pamela tried to explain, but she's kind of rough around the edges and harsh-spoken. Often when she's talking normally, she sounds like she's upset; add in parental anxiety and now this professional looking at her like he doesn't believe her, I imagine she didn't come off too well. At any rate, the doctor decided to report the incident to authorities, and the golden era in Pamela's life came to a painful end.

Pamela suffered through months of trials where her pre-sobriety past was brought out for all to judge, along with her brashness, and her cognitive disability, and the fact that she received support services from state and local agencies to help her with parenting. The judge weighed heavily the fact that Pamela had lost parental rights to two children earlier, and though there was no history of abuse or neglect with either of her current children, the court really felt that Pamela had purposely hit her son with the toy and saw this incident as a harbinger of trouble to come. Rights were terminated, and that was that.

Fast forward several years, to today. Both children have been adopted by the family who fostered them during Pamela's trials. Pamela has given birth three more times, each time with the child removed shortly after being born. She has been in and out of jail about a half dozen times, sometimes for drugs (her sobriety left about the same time her parental rights were terminated) and sometimes for domestic violence (her husband is still clean and has started divorce proceedings a number of times but each time decides he should stay).

Right about now, you may be wondering what happened to this book. We were going along so nicely with happy little vignettes describing quirky interactions with gloriously special people. Why stop here to unload this sad, depressing story? I tell it because this is reality in this ministry, and because sometimes you can pour in, you can come alongside, you can pray, and you can love, and you can try to pull along, but stuff still happens. People still choose poorly, and they get stuck in a seemingly endless loop of pain and darkness.

It's only seemingly endless, though, and there is real hope and real light. Pamela's story isn't over, and we really don't know everything about the inner landscape of her soul or her relationship with God. Remember also, that there are people who beat the odds and who do win on this side of heaven, with their lives transformed by God's love and His Word. We met some of these in Day 4. Our hope, though, is not found in a life turned around, and it's not found in people serving Him perfectly (Thank goodness, because I certainly don't!). Waiting until people seem to have it all together will keep you waiting a long time. Perfection is a myth, and anyone who chases it will miss moments like these:

5:51 p.m.
My laptop computer: *DING* notifying me of a new email. The message is from SmartJailMail.com, and it tells me that I have a new message from Pamela.

Pamela: "thank you for keeping me in your pray[er]s and im glad that you are doing well GOD and i bee[n] talking good things about you cant wait to see you when i get out have a blessed day GOD love[s] you"

As I read her words, I'm simultaneously encouraged and challenged in how I approach Father in prayer. Concerning the last few words, I know that she isn't just quoting a Christian slogan; she is speaking what she's heard from Him directly: "God loves you!" For Pamela, prayer is having a conversation with God, "talking good things" about people. When Pamela prays, she sets her own concerns aside, and the Spirit moves in her. She is transformed in the moment while she is completely focused on the person or situation she's praying for. I'm really glad to know she prays for me, and I will gladly and humbly accept this ministry from and through her as often as I can, and I won't wait until she's got her act together.

This goes for all of those we serve. If I chased and waited for perfection before I acknowledged God's work in His people, I'd miss treasures like this from another of my favorites (who am I kidding, they're all my favorites!):

10 p.m. Checking voicemails:
There's one at 2:08 p.m. from Michelle:
"(singing) STOP... for a minute...baby you're mine!
(speaking) Okay, uh...
(silence)
(more singing) Praise His naaaaaaame... Just praise His naaaaaaaaaame!...
(speaking again) I do...anyway, I do!
(silence)
So tell me, like, is that for real? Is there church this weekend? Like, is it for real? Get real, get real."
CLICK

This is how Michelle confirms that she would like a ride to church this weekend. Nobody does it like her, and I wouldn't have it any other way!

I love her desire to faithfully attend service, to be present with God's people in His house, lifting up His name. She's told me a number of times that Echo is a direct answer to prayer, as she had been so isolated, with no family nearby and no close friends. Michelle often has to fight schizophrenic torment to get to church; she battles voices telling her not to go and that people don't want her there. On top of this, her medications often make her tired or sick to her stomach, and then she forgets to eat and feels sick because of that. She does make it to church, though! Not every week, but most weeks she pulls it off, and I'm truly impressed and grateful!

11:10 p.m.
I head off to bed, singing: "Praise His naaaaaaame!"

Gathering Day: The Church Is Not a Building

12:05 p.m.

"Thank You, Jesus!" I mutter as the twenty-year-old church van fires up and stays running after a few attempts. As a bonus, the air conditioning appears to be working today, too. Things are looking up!

This week we're having our annual picnic at a local park, and as usual for food-related church gatherings, most of our folks are especially eager to attend. Since many of our people are unable to drive or otherwise obtain transportation every week, this means leaving early to pick them up. My first pick-up is Mary, who lives the greatest distance away, about twenty miles from my home.

12:40 p.m.

I pull up to the front door of Mary's nursing home. Leaving the van running, I hop out to set the step stool by the front passenger door and then ring the bell for the staff to let Mary out. Through the glass doors I see Mary, clutching her purse and taking a step backward and then a step forward, then looking over at the nurse and asking a question. The nurse nods reassuringly as she stands by the entrance, ready to enter the security code when Mary gets close enough to the door to open it.

12:50 p.m.

Mary squints and smiles up at the blue sky as she steps carefully through the door to the outside. "Ohhh," she exclaims. "It's a beautiful day, isn't it? Or, I shouldn't say 'isn't it' should I?"

"You're fine, honey! It's great to see you!" I move in for a quick hug, but "quick" and "Mary" don't usually come together, and the hug is tight and long-lasting. I don't mind; I imagine Mary doesn't get many hugs, so who am I to be stingy? Physical contact is especially important now with all the virus-related restrictions that have isolated this special population.

1:01 p.m.

We're now rolling on toward the next pick up. Keeping close watch on my driving, Mary asks in her sweet voice, "We're safe, right? You're a safe driver, aren't you, Rochelle?"

My response: "I sure do try!"

"We have nothing to fear..." she says quietly, almost to herself. Then, she brightly proclaims: "There's nothing to fear, because God is near!"

"You're so right, Mary!" We have a good laugh at her poetry. This is my favorite exchange with Mary because I know she struggles so much with fear. It's only been in the past couple of years that I've seen her start talking herself down from fear by reminding herself that she's not alone, and that God is with her.

1:35 p.m.
I call Michelle as I pull up to her apartment building.
When she picks up, I do my best Fonz: "Eyyyyyy!"

"Eyyyyyyyyyy!" Michelle's Fonz is much better than
mine.

"Hi, sweet-pea. I'm here!"

"Okay, bye!" *CLICK*

Michelle emerges momentarily, carrying her picnic
contribution along with a garbage bag full of empty re-
turnable soda cans and a second bag filled with clothes
to donate. Michelle is a very generous soul! I jump
down to put the step stool out for her and help her put
her things in the back of the van.

1:50 p.m.
Wilma climbs aboard, greeting everyone with a cheer-
ful, "Hi, honey!" She proceeds to chatter with Mary
and Michelle, asking how they are and how this or that
family member is doing.

1:55 p.m.
Danny & Joanna live in the same neighborhood, so
they're next. Curtis is on the porch waiting for us;
he rents from Danny & Joanna and often helps with
rides, but today he's riding with us. Partly to save
gas, but also, I believe, for the fellowship. He's tall
and strong and adds a quiet sense of security to any
outing. I roll down the window as he approaches and

thank him for having picked up Wednesday, who is following him down the steps off the porch. Curtis nods as he responds with his usual, "I got you, Pastor!" and climbs in.

Wednesday (that's the name she's chosen for herself) is dressed to the nines today with a pretty, black and white polka-dotted dress and a small vintage lace hat perched atop her curly purple hair. "Looking good, Wednesday!" I comment as she walks carefully down the uneven sidewalk.

She rewards me with one of her beautiful toothy grins, saying, "Why, thank you!"

When Danny pokes his head out the door, I holler, "Five minutes!" and he hollers back, "Okay! Okay!" and disappears.

2:10 p.m.
Finally, we pull away from Danny's house. Normally I would have left him behind, as I've done on a few occasions when he just couldn't get it together. Today, we're running a little ahead of schedule, so I cut him some slack. Joanna decided to stay home today since she's not feeling very well.

2:40 p.m.
We arrive at the park, where Lila has just pulled up with George and Nick from our Safe & Sound home. She's also picked up the pizza for us (thank goodness!), and within minutes, everyone has pitched in to move everything to the picnic tables. Nick's parents have arrived with his sister Becca, a local celebrity champion of those with special needs (herself, a

member of the elite Downs Syndrome crew); Becca is a favorite at Echo due to her boldness, terrific hugs, and encouragement offered from the purest heart. Blankets and chairs are spread out around the picnic tables, communion is prepared, and, once everyone is settled in, miracle of miracles, we're ready for service only a little after 3 p.m.!

We follow our regular service routine even though we're at a picnic. Routine is essential to providing an environment where people can pay attention to the Word; indeed, a predictable structure provides a blessed respite from lives often characterized by chaos. Our particular routine is pretty simple: we open with prayer and sing a song or two, we have time for announcements and offerings, we pray a blessing over the message, and then we have the message from Scripture. The sermons are usually more like Sunday school classes, as I ask a lot of questions to reinforce previous messages and to keep people engaged, and I leave a lot of room for their questions and comments. They are a naturally curious bunch, and they really want to understand what is being said. Their active involvement during this time is a testimony to their comfort level; they know that they are among friends and fellow pilgrims, and that it's safe to ask questions or to blurt out incorrect answers or to shrug and say, "I don't know!" Sometimes there's laughter, and it's not unheard of for us to pause a message, so we can gather around someone who is having a hard time emotionally, whether or not the issue is related to the message. After the sermon, we take communion, where we pause to reflect on the message and connect it with the work of Christ on the cross. Next comes one of my favorite parts, where individuals offer up prayers, either for themselves or others, and, after praying the Lord's prayer in unison, we conclude with one of our guys standing to read the Aaronic benediction from Numbers chapter 6. Everyone lifts their hands to receive the blessing from the Lord, and we finish with a resounding "Amen!" Since we're also eating today, I tack on my usual "...and thank You, God, for food!"

4:35 p.m.

While some are still visiting and eating, we start packing up the van to leave. By the time I get home this evening, I will have spent roughly seven hours transporting people to and from a one-hour church service. This used to concern me, as I felt like we could be so much more efficient with time and resources. I now know what many van ministry providers know: van ministry is about so much more than getting people from one place to another as quickly as possible. Very often, more ministry happens in the van than during the service. In the van, people care for each other and share their lives with one another. I'll sometimes overhear one person encouraging another with sincere Biblical counsel, and it's not uncommon for someone to offer a prayer when someone shares about a struggle they're having.

Of course, riding in the van is not always sunshine and

rainbows, especially if the air conditioning isn't working, or if the driver (usually me) is running late and
getting a little cranky. We've had to set some bound-
aries regarding garbage, verbal profanity, and general smelliness, and we've learned to keep a supply of
plastic bags handy in case there's a weak stomach on
board. We've also set time limits for those who habitu-
ally make others wait. All that aside, the van ministry
has helped us to experience church as something far
outside the building walls. The building, like the van, is
just a tool for us to be the church, gathering, and being
equipped to minister one to another.

6:15 p.m.
Wednesday, having her own reasons for wanting to
prolong her time away from home, has asked to ride
with me to take Mary home. She holds Mary's purse
while Mary lingers on the van's running board, one
foot hovering above the step stool which I'm sure
seems soooo far down. After shifting and turning a few
times, she looks over at me and says, "I'm sorry, just
get on with it, right?" I smile and let her know she's
fine. Once she's satisfied with her grip on the interior
handles, she lets gravity take her foot to the stool, and
it's just one more step down from there. "The eagle has
landed!" I exclaim, and Mary laughs with relief, taking
my hand as I walk her to the door.

The drive back to the city is pleasant. Sometimes
Wednesday and I chat; sometimes we ride in comfort-
able silence.

7:05 p.m.
"I love you, Wednesday! Be good! Make good choices!"

Wednesday gives me another of her lovely smiles as she turns away and calls over her shoulder, "Love you, too!"

I aim the van for home, tired, but full. I pat the van's dashboard saying, "Good job today!" It responds by cutting out the A/C. Well, at least it waited until all my passengers were gone!

Rest Day: Rest Like You Believe God Can Handle It

6:55 a.m.
I open one eye, note that the sun hasn't fully risen yet, remember it's my rest day, and promptly drop back off to sleep.

7:50 a.m.
From a deep sleep, I awaken to Paco, one of my cats, crying for breakfast. I roll over after mumbling something about being right there, and I hear his feet padding away to the kitchen.

9:15 a.m.
I open both eyes to see my other cat, Princess, staring at me intently. Paco is by the door, and once he notices I'm awake, he resumes his plaintive cries for food. He doesn't leave the doorway this time until I'm actually up and moving toward the kitchen.

In all honesty, this is fairly early for me to be getting up on a Sunday. Since our services are on Saturdays, I take my day off on Sunday, and it typically starts with a lot of sleep. Throughout the day, I may take care of emails or even a little paperwork, and I usually go visit my parents for a few hours. The keys to embracing this time of rest are being unhurried in everything I'm doing, and having the phone on Do Not Disturb or even turned off altogether. I've let the congregation know that I won't generally take or return any calls on Sunday, and for the most part, they do a terrific job honoring that boundary. Even my wards know that, if there's an emergency during this time, they ought to go ahead and call 911, as emergency services will be able to help them more quickly than I would. Do I nail it perfectly every week? No, but generally speaking, rest and family time are the rule on Sundays, and church work is the exception.

It's taken me a number of years to get to this point, as for a long time I felt like I was obligated to be available every day. Early in my ministry, at the insistence of the church's board and in acknowledgement of my limitations, I started to set some time aside for rest, but I generally managed to fill that time with some type of work that I felt had to be done that day. Eventually, I realized that I was basically acting as though I didn't believe God could handle things while I rested! It sounds silly, but it's really what we're doing when we think we need to be available twenty-four hours a day, seven days a week.

Today, rest is more than fulfilling a commandment or following my board's direction, or even an investment in self-care. More than anything, it's an act of faith, indicating to God that I believe He's got it all under control. He really can handle it! It's also a beautiful time devoted to drawing close to God and experiencing His presence in quietness and unhurriedness. I urge all ministers to have and to guard their rest time with the Lord, as it's from this well that we draw strength and passion for serving the way we do.

On that note, I think now is a good time to start to wrap up our time together. I've offered you only the tiniest peek into the lives of just a handful of our people; there's so much more I could share about these precious souls, and there are others, as well, that I haven't even mentioned. Some who know us might read this and wonder how I could have missed highlighting our own "Mother Theresa," whom we know as Sister Love, and her adult foster girls: Mary Ann, who, though nonverbal, can easily communicate joy and concern and humor and love for Jesus; Debbie Lynn, whose prayers could move the stodgiest people to tears; and Vickie, whose love for anything purple has earned her the nickname "Purple People Eater" and who, simply and sweetly, took up the mantle of prayer when Debbie Lynn developed Alzheimer's Disease (as often happens with people who live with Down's Syndrome) before passing softly out of our lives and into the arms of her Savior. Some might also wonder how I could forget to mention my own dad, who recently suffered a massive stroke and has entered the realm of the disabled, requiring twenty-four--hour care and struggling mightily, but faithfully insisting on participating in a nightly hour-long prayer call, and patiently listening to me when I share with him about concerns I have with the church. His voice is barely over a whisper most of the time, and I usually have to ask him to repeat himself, but it's worth the effort because he offers sound wisdom and prayers filled with hope and sincere belief that this is God's church. Or what about Lloyd, a recent addition from the nearby senior home, holding out the last note of every song as he grips his walker tightly to hold up his tiny, cerebral-palsy-twisted frame. "I learned how to sing like that from singing with the Brightmoor Tabernacle Church choir in Detroit!" Finally, as suggested by my pastoral coach, I could have shared my own story of overcoming mental illness and finding healing in relationship with my heavenly Father; this aspect of my relationship with God indeed fuels and informs much of my ministry passion today.

Perhaps these stories, and many others, will yet be told, if not by me, then by someone else. I trust that the stories I did share are the ones that needed to be told at this time. At the very least, I hope you've enjoyed going on this treasure hunt with me, and perhaps even found yourself itching to get started on your own adventure! If that's the case, stick around for several more pages while I share some suggestions for getting started. This is, by no means, meant to be an exhaustive resource; I only intend to share some steps that you may find helpful.

Getting Started

Step 0: Pray

I confess, I listed the three steps below long before I thought to put in this one! If you already have in your heart the desire to reach those with disabilities, I believe it's quite likely that God placed that desire there, and He is ready to give you direction and provision. Make and keep prayer a regular part of your work, and God will guide you. Be sure to enlist all of the prayer warriors you know, because this is a mighty work!

Step 1: Assess the Need

While some aspects of special needs ministry will be universal, every region and every person are unique. I encourage you to do your research, make phone calls, ask questions, and, in all your planning, consider staying local (especially if you're small, like we are!). I assure you, you'll find plenty of need in your own area! Here are some places to start asking questions:

- Your church: Many already know people with disabilities and/or mental illness and will have ideas about how to reach them.

- Local government: For example, we regularly lead prayer at our local township hall meetings, and this led to us hosting a large, well-established AA group.

Most officials are happy to hear about people willing to serve and may have connections with needs that you don't know about.

- Senior homes: Some are well-served by local churches, and some have no interest in church involvement, but many are desperately under-served, and their people are hungry for connection. We serve communion monthly at a local home and, though we are small and don't offer a huge ministry there, this small regular touch is felt and appreciated deeply, and the residents are starting to be formed into their own little congregation.

- Group or Adult Foster Care (AFC) homes: These can be found by doing a search of your state's government website for licensed facilities. Reach out first to the owners of the homes, as calling the homes directly can aggravate already overworked staff (Some of our community's unsung heroes!). Some homes will be very guarded and may even reject your offer; thank them for their time and move on, because others will be very open and happy you reached out.

- Local agencies serving the mentally ill and disabled: We have several agencies serving this population in our area, and their case managers are another group of some of the most under-appreciated heroes. You may initially have contact with them through one of their recipients, but I've found that they are also generally open to receiving cold calls from ministries seeking ways to help.

- Hospital social workers: Another group of heroes I have encountered are the hospital social workers. They are very aware of the needs of people passing through their hands, and they could provide some good ideas for how you can serve.

- Your county's probate court: Many adults with disabilities have guardians appointed by a probate court; you may find it useful to connect with the court administrators.

- Jail or prison chaplaincy offices: It's a heartbreaking reality that many cognitively challenged and/or mentally ill adults find themselves in jail at some point; the chaplain may have ideas for how you can help these vulnerable individuals during and after incarceration.

Step 2: Decide What to Offer

Based on your prayerful research, consider how your group could realistically serve. The list below contains some things that we've done, and some that we haven't.

- Prayer: You can adopt a home for prayer, whether or not you let them know.

- Gift baskets for homes and/or individuals: We haven't had any group refuse a holiday gift basket! You might even adopt a resident to provide birthday gifts or other special attention. You could ask a home if there's anyone who doesn't receive visits and focus on that person. Also, you could consider providing appreciation gifts for staff; happy staff can mean happier residents!

- In-home Bible studies or worship services: You can keep this simple, with a short message, songs, prayer, and communion, if appropriate.

- Community meals programs: We have a Love INC chapter (www.loveinc.org) in our area that offers community meals where different churches host and serve food. Perhaps you could host or provide volunteers to serve at such a meal; it's a great opportunity to connect with people, many of whom are lonely and/or have special needs.

- A delivered meal: Group homes are also generally grateful to receive food delivered; you will probably want to develop relationship with them first in order to build trust, but it can be a great blessing and opportunity for outreach to order a delivery pizza once in a while!

- Rides to church: As you saw in the Gathering Day chapter, transportation is a huge part of our ministry. We found that, while special needs individuals, especially those in group homes, have recipient rights that entitle them to transportation to church, for various reasons it is difficult to make that transportation happen consistently. It's a huge blessing and witness to the home to offer that transportation. If you don't have a van, you might consider setting up a driver rotation where individuals in your church each agree to pick up at least one person one or more times a month. You could also look at budgeting for Uber or Lyft or other transportation services available in your area; we did that until we had our vans, and if you're picking up more than one person from a household, it's really pretty cost-efficient.

- A service time that accommodates special needs: You may have noticed in the Gathering Day chapter that our service time is non-traditional, as we meet on Saturdays at 3 p.m. Our meeting time evolved from a regular Sunday morning meeting to wanting to have a monthly evening meal, which we would do on Saturdays at 6 p.m. This then changed to Saturday evening meetings every week, but when we started to have more special needs individuals attending, we found that this time was difficult due to meals and medications. Mornings are very difficult for caregiving families and home staff, especially when there's more than one individual to get ready, so we landed on 3 p.m. as our "sweet spot" because it gives people plenty of time to get ready after lunch, nobody misses dinner, and people mostly don't have meds until later. Be willing to experiment; the Scripture does not mandate that we meet on Sunday mornings. It really doesn't.

- Outings: Though these can be stressful and are usually exhausting, they are also almost always great fun and can actually be quite simple to accomplish. Some examples: shopping for groceries (remember, many don't have transportation and many also don't live near an affordable grocery store); movie nights; coffee; meals; retreats; walks (we participate in an annual a CROP Walk every year, and our wheeled members love it!); hayrides/farms/cider mills (these are big here in Michigan); sports events.

- Your building: What do I mean by this? There are agencies that serve the special needs community in day-camp settings that may need extra space, especially with social distancing requirements in place during the COVID-19 pandemic. We partner with a farm that trains individuals and helps them maximize their abilities, and they needed extra space this summer; they have been able to use our building for this, and as a bonus, this has helped fund our ministry. This can be especially useful since with a growing special needs congregation you may find more of your income will need to come from outside your fellowship!

Step 3: Get Equipped

Here I want to emphasize that this is not intended to be a comprehensive resource; I'm sure to miss something that you may find essential! Please accept this list for what it is, just some suggestions for preparing yourself to serve the special needs community.

- Assess your "disability friendliness": There are a lot of resources online that provide great check lists and even assessments for determining how ready your church is to serve those with special needs. Two great websites I've found are www.specialtouch.org and www.keyministry.com.

- Consider accessibility aids and building updates: There's a wide variety of ways to make your building and services more accessible. I suggest you start with ADA compliance and move on to wheelchair and other mobility equipment and visual aids, such as large print and/or braille materials. Depending on the population you are serving, you could designate a sensory room (similar to a cry room) that an individual could inconspicuously retreat to if they are being over stimulated.

- Training: Thankfully, there are many resources available for in-person or online training, some of which are offered by local community agencies. Where possible, I suggest going with local training, as it provides a great opportunity to network with people in the field. Here are some suggested trainings:

    - First Aid/CPR: This is a good idea for any church, but medical incidents are especially common among special needs individuals, and you or your staff should be prepared to stabilize a situation while waiting for professional help to arrive.

- Mental Health First Aid: This is a tremendously helpful training for any who encounter individuals suffering with mental illness, which is today, everybody! You can find online or in-person training at www.mentalhealthfirstaid.org.

- Culture of Gentleness/Gentle Teaching: I learned about this training while writing this book (special thanks to Toni Ufolla, who performed a diligent review of this material and provided some wonderful suggestions). I have since taken the introductory class and I can't recommend it enough! Read more about it and find available courses at www.gentleteaching.com.

- Insurance: Consult your insurance agent regarding any special riders you might need in your policy. If you don't have an insurance agent, please, please get one!

- Laws in your state and community: You may want to know what rights individuals with disabilities have, such as what's included in the Americans with Disabilities Act, what recipient rights are, what guardians are responsible for, what it means to petition for hospitalization or evaluation of an individual, and the process for filing complaints or concerns with Adult or Child Protective Services. These can be helpful when serving someone who has a lot of complaints because you can assure them of their rights and also help them understand where they may need to adjust their expectations. For example, I was surprised to learn that a guardian is only responsible to see their ward once every three months, and to report to the court only once a year. Many wards hope for more of a parenting relationship from their guardians, and in some cases, they may receive that, but it's not a legal right that they can demand. Oh, and you'll also want to know if there are any legal concerns with any of the ministry you're providing. You know, for liability and such… your insurance agent will be able to help with that as well!

- Transportation: There are a lot of options here! Individuals can provide transportation with limited liability, but you could also go for a twelve- or fifteen-passenger van modified with ramps, steps, or handles. At least in Michigan, no special license is required to drive a fifteen-passenger van, but you may want to carefully vet and train your van drivers, both in how to drive a full van (it feels quite different from driving an empty van or a smaller vehicle) as well as for handling special people while driving under stressful conditions. We have some decent drivers in our church, but not all of them have the temperament for van ministry!

- Outreach to and partnering with other churches/ministries: The farm I mentioned earlier is an example of this. We've also found some great connections with other churches in our local Love INC (www.loveinc.org) chapter. As with some group homes or nursing homes, be prepared to encounter some barriers; in some cases, the administrators are (understandably) just protecting their people, but in some cases, you'll find leaders wanting to protect their ministries. Thank them for their time and move on; there may be a connection later, but you don't have to force one now. There will be plenty of others who will want to partner with you!

And now, my friend, it's time for us to part company. I've given you a map and some shovels, and the assurance that there is gold in these hills. The next steps are up to you. Maybe we'll meet again in the field! Until then, God's blessings on you as you continue to serve Him faithfully.

About the Author

Reverend Rochelle Beckemeyer has served as senior pastor at Echo Christian Fellowship in Lake Orion, MI, since June of 2008, having received a Master of Divinity degree from Michigan Theological Seminary and ordination credentials through the Assemblies of God. In addition to serving in ministry, Rochelle works full time providing systems support in the automotive industry and serves as guardian to five mentally ill adults. She is mom to an adopted daughter (now adult) with whom she founded a separate nonprofit corporation, Safe & Sound Ministries, to improve the quality of life of special needs individuals. This book was written to raise awareness of and encourage participation in ministry with this special population, and all proceeds will benefit Safe & Sound Ministries. Pastor Rochelle is available to speak with you, your board, or your congregation about serving this special population and helping you to do the same! Reach out to her ministry any time at contact@ safensoundministries.com.